S0-CPE-944

The Unexpected

Program Authors

Connie Juel, Ph.D.

Jeanne R. Paratore, Ed.D.

Deborah Simmons, Ph.D.

Sharon Vaughn, Ph.D.

PEARSON
Scott
Foresman

Glenview, Illinois
Boston, Massachusetts
Chandler, Arizona
Upper Saddle River, New Jersey

ISBN-13: 978-0-328-45297-2
ISBN-10:   0-328-45297-1

8 9 10 V011 14 13
CC1

The Unexpected

Marvelous MISHAPS 5

How can unplanned situations lead to positive outcomes?

CHANGING NATURE 31

What unexpected effects can humans have on nature?

Contents

Marvelous MISHAPS

Words 2 the Wise

Situations and events don't always turn out the way we plan or expect them to. As you read, think about how an unplanned or **unexpected situation** can be a positive thing.

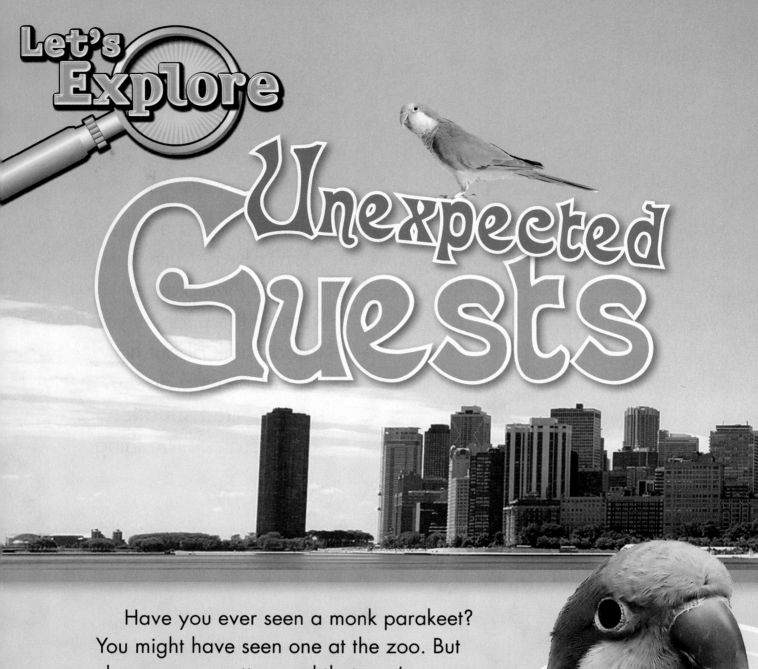

Let's Explore

Unexpected Guests

Have you ever seen a monk parakeet? You might have seen one at the zoo. But chances are pretty good that you've never encountered one in your backyard. Why is that? These small, tropical birds usually make their home in South America!

But here is a surprise. You can see monk parakeets in Chicago, Illinois! About 200 of these unexpected guests make their home in parks on the city's south side.

Monk parakeets live in parts of South America that are warm year-round.

How did parakeets from South America find their way to the Midwest? The Chicago colony* got its start in 1973. At that time, large numbers of these birds were being shipped to the United States as pets. Some of these birds probably escaped from pet stores or private homes. Others may have been released. Once free, the birds found a place to nest and settled into their new home.

*colony living things of the same kind that grow or live together in a group

Not many people would predict that these birds could survive the harsh winters of the Midwest. But each year the Chicago parakeets put up with howling winds, freezing rain, snowstorms, and temperatures below zero. Brrr! Why don't the parakeets fly south like many of their feathered friends? Monk parakeets don't migrate. They live in one place year-round.

Winters in Chicago can be a challenge for people as well as parakeets.

10

Chicago's monk parakeets make nests in tree branches, on utility poles, and even on satellite dishes.

How have these tropical birds managed to survive? They build huge nests that are home to several families. Each family enters through its own hole at the bottom of the nest. It's not much different from an apartment building for people! These nests are advantageous because they keep the birds warm and dry. During the coldest months, people also put out food for the parakeets. Chicagoans would be disappointed if their unexpected guests did not feel welcome!

Discoveries!

by Amie Jane Leavitt

Have you ever made a mistake? That's okay. Mistakes are part of life. People make them every day. But not all mistakes are bad. Some mistakes are advantageous. Some of the world's greatest inventions are the result of mistakes.

Oops!

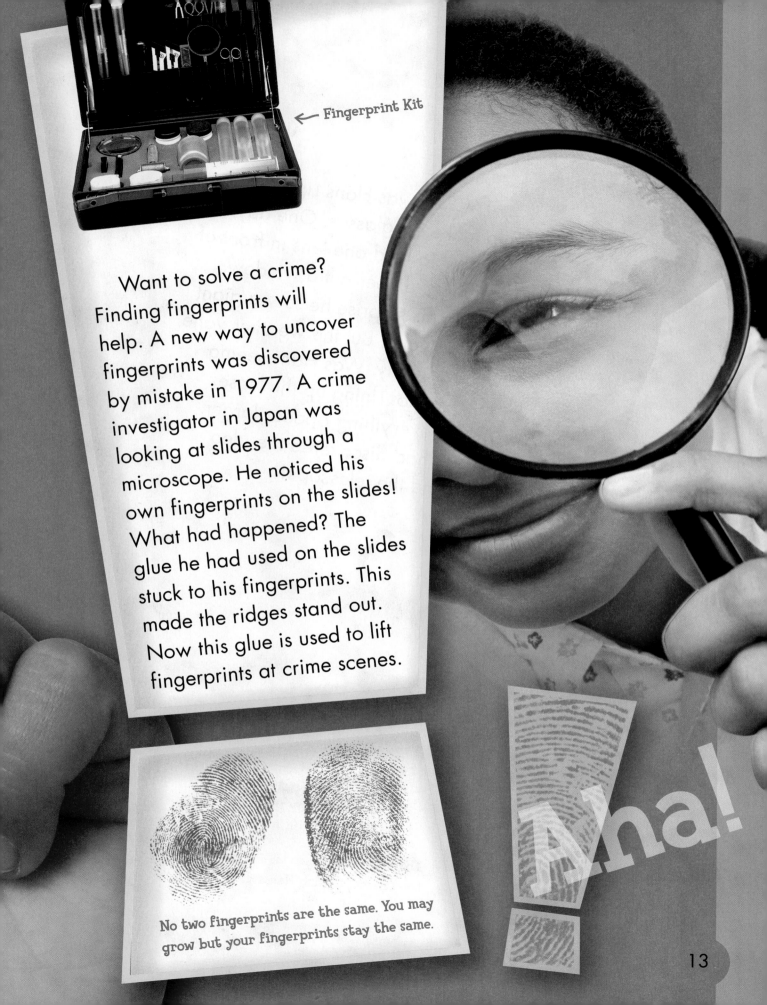

← Fingerprint Kit

Want to solve a crime? Finding fingerprints will help. A new way to uncover fingerprints was discovered by mistake in 1977. A crime investigator in Japan was looking at slides through a microscope. He noticed his own fingerprints on the slides! What had happened? The glue he had used on the slides stuck to his fingerprints. This made the ridges stand out. Now this glue is used to lift fingerprints at crime scenes.

No two fingerprints are the same. You may grow but your fingerprints stay the same.

Aha!

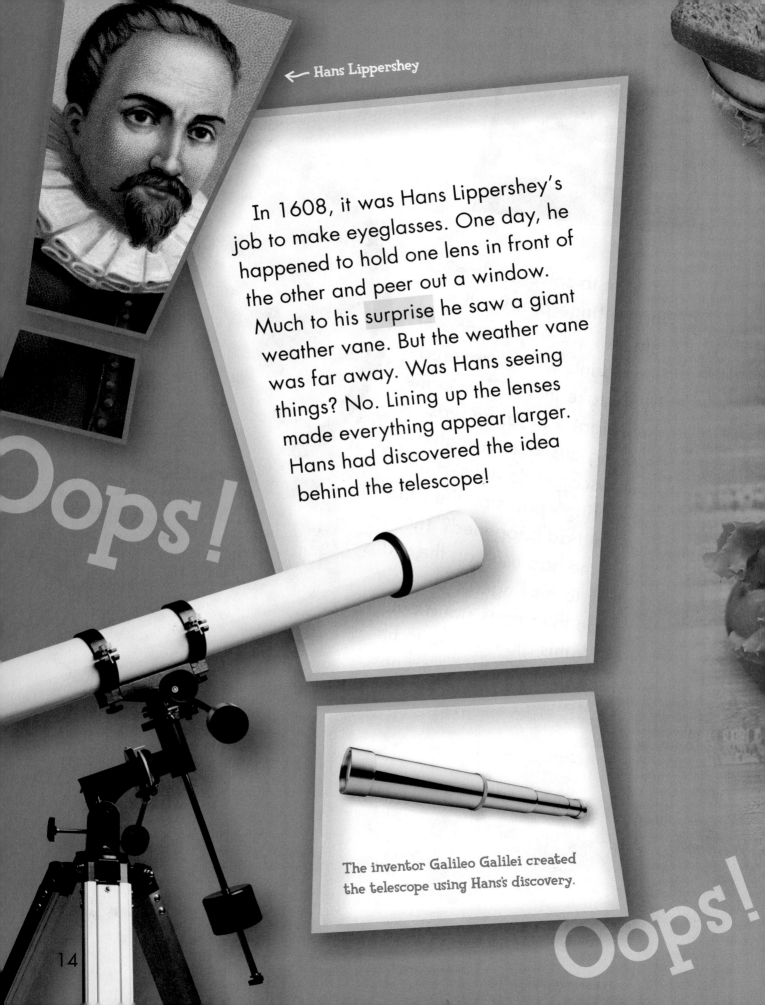

← Hans Lippershey

In 1608, it was Hans Lippershey's job to make eyeglasses. One day, he happened to hold one lens in front of the other and peer out a window. Much to his surprise he saw a giant weather vane. But the weather vane was far away. Was Hans seeing things? No. Lining up the lenses made everything appear larger. Hans had discovered the idea behind the telescope!

Oops!

The inventor Galileo Galilei created the telescope using Hans's discovery.

Oops!

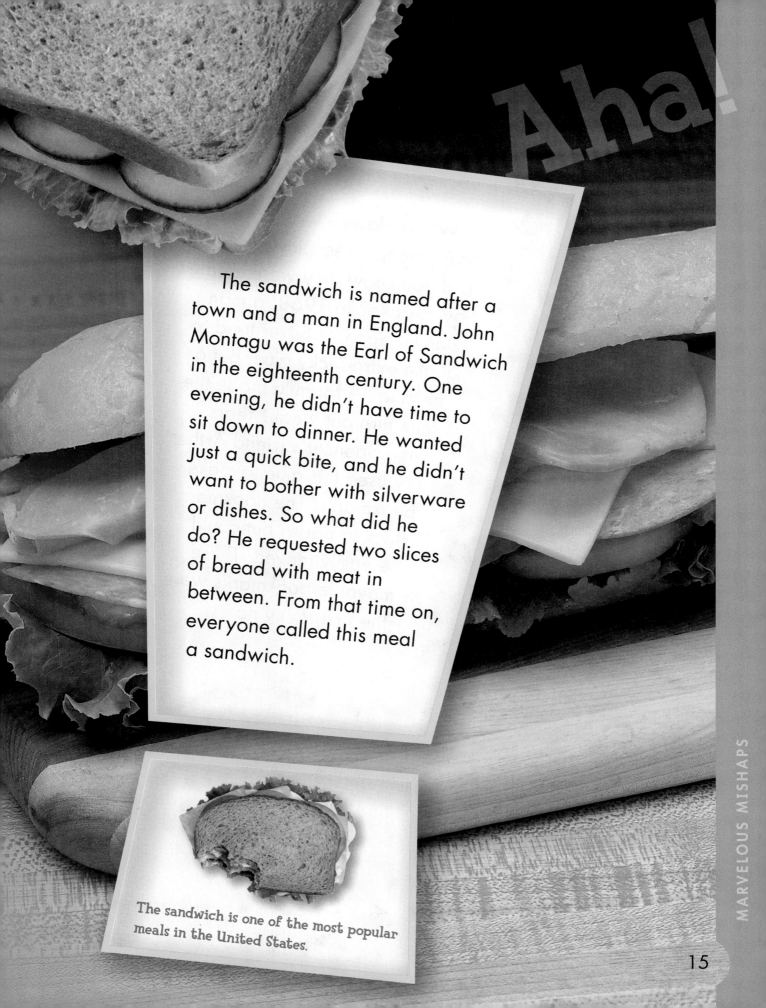

The sandwich is named after a town and a man in England. John Montagu was the Earl of Sandwich in the eighteenth century. One evening, he didn't have time to sit down to dinner. He wanted just a quick bite, and he didn't want to bother with silverware or dishes. So what did he do? He requested two slices of bread with meat in between. From that time on, everyone called this meal a sandwich.

The sandwich is one of the most popular meals in the United States.

← Arthur Fry

Where do you write little notes? Many people use sticky notes. Did you know they were created by mistake? In 1968, a man named Spencer Silver tried to make extra-sticky glue. But a hitch in his formula made the glue turn out weak. Years later, Spencer's friend Arthur Fry used this glue to make bookmarks. The bookmarks stuck to pages but could be easily moved. These movable bookmarks were the first sticky notes!

Oops!

Sticky notes come in many shapes and sizes.

Alexander Fleming was a scientist who studied germs. In 1928, he was experimenting with bacteria that caused deadly infections. Though he took the usual precautions, some mold got into a dish of bacteria. Alexander thought his experiment was ruined. But later he observed that a space had formed between the mold and the bacteria. The mold was killing the bacteria! This mistake led to the discovery of penicillin.

Penicillin is a drug that has saved many lives.

Aha!

Another discovery comes to us through an Arabian legend. A man was traveling across the desert. He carried a bag filled with milk. Midway through his journey, he peered into the bag and encountered a surprise. The milk was thick and full of chunks. Tasting it, the man found it to be delightful. On a hot and dusty road, he had discovered how to make cheese!

Cheese is made from milk that is allowed to spoil. The milk may come from cows or goats.

Oops!

Moo!

Frank Epperson was 11 years old in 1905. One evening, he used a wooden stick to mix his favorite drink of soda powder and water. Frank left the drink in his backyard overnight. The next morning, he discovered that the stick had frozen in the drink. Was Frank disappointed? No. He simply pulled the frozen drink out of the cup. Many years later, this became a popular treat.

Next time you make a mistake, don't worry. It might result in an unintended discovery!

What Do You Think?

Which mistake led to the most useful discovery? Why do you think so?

Aha!

Back to Nature!

by Stephanie Tejeda • illustrated by Dani Jones

The travel brochure sounded too good to be true.

"Look," Dad said. "Get back to nature at beautiful Surprise Lake!"

Dad found the brochure in Joe's Auto Repair. Joe was fixing our car—again. The brochure showed a sparkling, blue lake surrounded by tall pine trees. Kids were splashing around in the water. Mom and I had to admit that it did look nice.

"Swimming, hiking, fishing, and much more!" Dad exclaimed. "We'll even have our own cabin on the lake!"

Joe said that our car could make the trip to Surprise Lake without a hitch. He should know. He's replaced every part of our car except the windshield wipers.

"Back to nature!" Dad shouted as we pulled onto the highway.

Midway through our journey, nature got back at us. We ran into a huge storm. Blankets of water hit the windshield. And guess what? The windshield wipers didn't work! Dad's face turned red. Mom's face twisted.

We had to pull over. We ate lunch. Then Dad and I played chess. Mom read her book. Three hours later the rain finally stopped. We were on our way again.

Dad was disappointed that we weren't on schedule, but who can predict problems?

Later that night, we arrived at Surprise Lake. It was down a bumpy, unpaved road. It was really dark. An old man with a lantern greeted us.

"Howdy folks!" he shouted. "Welcome to Surprise!"

"Hello," Dad said. "Did the electricity go out?"

"No, sir," the old man laughed. "Don't have electricity. That's why the brochure says *back to nature.*"

"Now I see why they call it *Surprise,*" Mom joked. The old man showed us to our cabin.

"Isn't this great?" Dad exclaimed upon entering the log cabin.

"The bugs certainly seem to think so," said Mom. "There must be a million of them."

Dad set the lantern on the table. Mom sprayed for bugs.

The next morning we woke to the sound of a loud bell. "Come and get it!" someone shouted. We struggled out of our hammocks like flies in a spider web.

We walked outside to see the morning sun sparkling on the lake. A big table of food was in the yard. We and five other families sat down to an unusual country breakfast. There were things like catfish omelets and possum stew. Another surprise. It tasted good!

Later that day we decided to go fishing. Mom and I rowed an old, wooden boat. Dad put worms on our hooks and sang songs. We were way over on the other side of the lake before we noticed that our feet were getting wet.

"I think there's a hole in the boat!" I shouted.

The water started coming in fast. Dad was scooping it out with a cup. Mom was rowing like crazy to the shore.

Once ashore, we whistled and shouted for help, but no one could hear us. "There must be a trail around here," Dad said. "We'll just walk back."

Mom and I tried not to show that we were disappointed or afraid. So we laughed and fought our way through the bushes and trees. Finally we found a trail.

The forest was beautiful. We saw birds, rabbits, butterflies, and, of course, insects. We were really enjoying ourselves, until we saw a bear!

"Run!" Mom shouted. I never knew my parents could run so fast. Later, out of breath and energy, we stopped. The bear wasn't following us.

"Isn't it great to get back to nature?" Dad said.

We laughed and joked all the way back to camp. Our vacation didn't go without a hitch, but we did have a great time.

"You can't always predict what's going to happen," Mom said. "But that's part of the fun!"

What Do You Think?

Did the family enjoy their trip? How do you know?

BIRD WATCHING

by *Beverly McLoughland*

I went bird watching
And what did I see,
Sitting on a limb
Of a linden tree?
A fat, little
Black-capped
Chickadee,
Looking through binoculars
Back at me.

Daddy Fell into the Pond

by Alfred Noyes

Everyone grumbled. The sky was gray.
We had nothing to do and nothing to say.
We were nearing the end of a dismal day,
And there seemed to be nothing beyond,
            THEN
Daddy fell into the pond!

And everyone's face grew merry and bright,
And Timothy danced for sheer delight,
"Give me the camera, quick, oh quick!
He's crawling out of the duckweed." *Click!*

Then the gardener suddenly slapped his knee,
And doubled up, shaking silently,
And the ducks all quacked as if they were daft
And it sounded as if the old drake laughed.

O, there wasn't a thing that didn't respond
            WHEN
Daddy fell into the pond!

4 YOU 2 DO

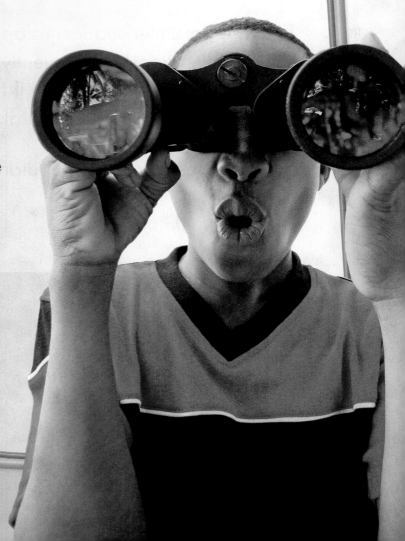

Word Play

How many words can you make by adding a prefix from column one to a base word in column two?

post-   appear
pre-   pay
re-   view
dis-   night
mid-   date

Making Connections

How might one of the people in "Discoveries!" react to the unexpected events in "Back to Nature"?

On Paper

Write about a time when something unexpected happened to you. What was the outcome?

Answers for Word Play: postdate, prepay,
preview, predate, reappear, repay, review,
disappear, midnight

CHANGING NATURE

Contents

CHANGING NATURE

Let's Explore

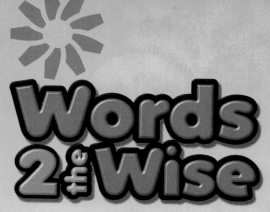

Words 2 the Wise

Humans' effect on nature can be good or bad. As you read, think about how your actions might cause changes in nature in a positive or negative way.

HOOVER DAM

A dam is a wall that holds back the water of a stream or river. Dams can provide electricity. The water can also be used for drinking and farming.

The Hoover Dam was built above the Colorado River in 1932. The dam was completed in 1935. The project amazed people all over the world.

There is enough concrete in the Hoover Dam to pave a highway from New York to San Francisco!

Some said the project was necessary. Businesses would thrive where there used to be just canyon and desert.

But others thought there was too much to lose. They didn't want to fill a beautiful canyon with all that water.

The Hoover Dam is considered a wonder of the world. The dam provides power and water to many who need it. Some still wonder if losing the canyon was worth it.

Lake Mead was formed when the Hoover Dam was built. Nine million people visit Lake Mead every year.

Hoover Dam is 726 feet tall. It weighs 6,600,000 tons. About 16,000 people worked on building the dam.

THE "MILE-A-MINUTE PLANT"

by Alexander Day

How would you like to have a plant outside your window called the "foot-a-night vine"? If so, go ahead and plant kudzu (KOOD-zoo).

But if you put kudzu in your garden, you could be in trouble. Kudzu can grow up to a foot a day. In one season, it can grow over 60 feet long! Kudzu grows best in the southeastern part of the United States. It's now considered a pest from Georgia to Illinois.

The Gift of an Amazing Plant

That wasn't always the case. Kudzu was considered a treasure when it was first brought to this country.

The year was 1876. A 100th anniversary celebration of the Declaration of Independence was held in Philadelphia, Pennsylvania. Nations from all over the world built exhibits in honor of our country's birthday. Japan created an amazing garden that was filled with kudzu. The leaves grew large and the flowers smelled like grapes!

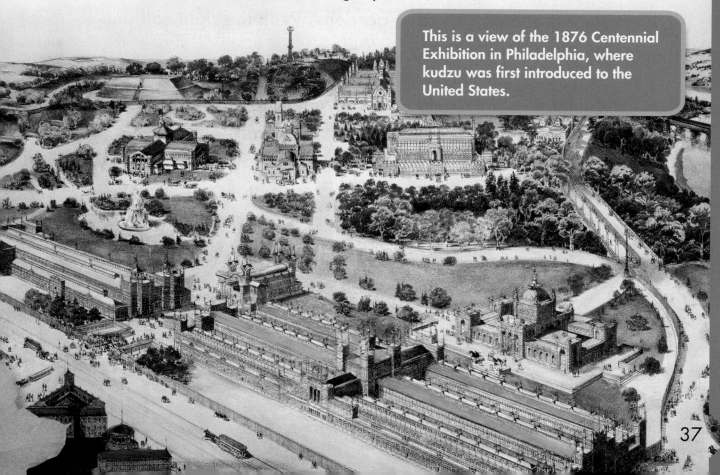

This is a view of the 1876 Centennial Exhibition in Philadelphia, where kudzu was first introduced to the United States.

Kudzu has attractive leaves, and the flowers have a sweet smell.

Growing Fast

American gardeners went on to plant kudzu because the plant looked nice in gardens. With the right soil and weather, kudzu really took off.

Businesses here began to promote it too. Seed companies in Florida sold kudzu through the mail. They told farmers it was good food for animals.

One radio commentator did broadcasts from his front porch. He promoted kudzu as a crop that "works while you sleep." Farmers planted over a million acres.

It survived so well because Japanese people didn't bring over any of the plant's insect enemies. Without natural enemies, kudzu could thrive in its new habitat.

Going Out of Control

Pretty soon kudzu started taking over. People discovered that kudzu kills other plants. It does this by covering and smothering them. The vines help keep the soil in place. But kudzu destroys forests by blocking sunlight. In 1953, the U.S. Department of Agriculture declared kudzu a pest weed.

An abandoned cabin in Georgia during the spring. Kudzu vines are just starting to climb.

Kudzu now contaminates up to seven million acres. It's not easy to get rid of kudzu either. Some kudzu plants take ten years to kill.

Farmers tried to get rid of kudzu by mowing it like grass. To control the vine, farmers had to destroy it at the root. Even if the plant has gone above ground, the root can continue to grow underground.

Kudzu grows quickly and covers everything in its path.

Kudzu vines have covered this building in Georgia.

Kudzu contamination is costly. It completely replaces whatever plants were there before. A land owner might spend more than $1,000 per acre over five years to control kudzu.

Kudzu was originally planted to make the yard around a home look attractive. Now it often covers crumbling old houses in the South. Trees covered with kudzu look like big green bears.

Living With It

Scientists are trying to use kudzu. One university has raised Angora goats in fields of kudzu. The goats eat the plant and keep it from spreading further. Then the goats can produce milk and wool to be sold.

Some people believe that since it thrives here, it can be made useful. Craft artists find that the rubbery vines are excellent for making baskets. A woman in Alabama makes over 200 kudzu baskets each year. People call her "The Queen of Kudzu."

People are starting to find ways to use kudzu vines.

Nancy Basket uses kudzu vines to make baskets.

An artist named Nancy Basket makes paper and baskets from kudzu. The paper is used in art projects.

One cook uses kudzu in many recipes. Deep-fried kudzu leaves are a favorite. Ground kudzu root is called kuzu in China and Japan. It has been used in cooking and medicine for centuries.

Kudzu started out as a gift. Then it became a problem. Kudzu can be useful, but if it is growing near you, you'd better close the windows at night!

WHAT DO YOU THINK?

Why did kudzu become a problem in the United States? How have people tried to solve it?

Natural WONDERS

by Tim Prentiss

If you could take a trip to see nature at its best, where would you go? Maybe you'd want to paddle down cool rivers. Maybe you'd climb a mountain or take a swim with tropical fish near a coral reef. Maybe you'd play on a sandy beach.

Let's take a look at beautiful sites in the world! But your trip will be more than a vacation. You'll find out how tourists affect nature.

Orangutans in Sumatra

Mountains in Nepal

Coral reef in Jamaica

Coral Reefs
WONDERLAND OR WASTELAND?

Dive into warm, tropical water. See what awaits you below! Here, coral reefs are homes to almost one million species of fish, crabs, eels, mollusks, sponges, worms, grasses, and algae.

Clownfish and porcupine fish swim past. Bright yellows, blues, and reds of deep-sea animals light the way. Snap a picture of the lionfish and float back up to the surface.

Lionfish

Sea anemones (uh-NEM-uh-neez) and fish live together in this coral reef.

Coral is a living thing! There are only 368,000 square miles of coral reefs in the ocean. All the creatures that call a reef home depend on each other to survive. When one part of the reef is damaged, other living parts can die. Coral reefs can become extinct.

Too Much Algae

- Algae grow in coral reefs.
- Human sewage and pesticides* promote algae growth.
- Too much algae can smother coral.

*pesticides chemicals used to kill harmful bugs

The Spotted Trunkfish swims through a coral reef.

The Elkhorn coral is now in danger in the coral reefs of the Caribbean.

A Majestic Mountain or a Junkyard?

Travel to Nepal for a great adventure. Join a team and climb Mount Everest. It is the highest mountain in the world. It is located in the Himalayan Mountain range.

Climbers need protective clothing, equipment, and trained guides. The hike is risky!

You may not plan to climb to the top, but even at the foot of the mountain, you'll be close to a wonder of nature.

Mount Everest rises 29,035 feet high.

Once Mount Everest was untouched. Now more and more climbers try to reach the top each year. As they go, they dump climbing equipment, oxygen tanks, tents, and other garbage. Now the mountain is full of trash. Few clean-up crews pick up trash. Tourists have changed what the mountain looks like.

- About 900 mountain climbers trek the highest peaks each year.
- About 40,000 other climbers visit the lower peaks.

Between 1950 and 1990 about 50 tons of trash has piled up on Mount Everest.

Saving Sumatran Orangutans

Tourists can visit natural spots without harming the landscape or animals. In fact some tourists go where they will help animals. Tourists to the island of Sumatra can visit a forest where orangutans (uh-RANG-uh-tans) live. Tourists watch orangutans eat bananas and swing from branches. These tourists sleep in hammocks at night. The money from these tourists helps preserve the orangutans' habitat.

Sasa and Bruno are two of the orangutans at the Sumatran Orangutan Society preserve.

Protect It from Home

What is your favorite place in nature? Is it a river? a snowy peak? a northern lake? You can help preserve natural places at home.

Find out about places that you are interested in. Learn more about how people affect these places. Then be a friend to the Earth.

What can you do to protect your favorite place?

Be a Friend to the Earth

- Learn about the wonders of the Earth. Future generations depend on you!
- Try to buy products that are made from recycled materials. This helps reduce waste.
- Can you reduce air pollution? Yes! Cool down by opening the windows. Limit air conditioning.
- If you travel, clean up after yourself! Put trash in a container.

Remember, the wise traveler takes only photographs and leaves only footprints.

What Do You Think?

How do humans affect nature?

Are You a Danger to Nature?

Test your knowledge on how to make the Earth cleaner.

1. Which of these activities causes air pollution?

    a. riding a bike
    b. letting a faucet drip
    c. driving a car

2. You and your mom are waiting in the car for your brother to get out of school. The car's engine is running. What would help keep the air cleaner?

    a. Leave the air conditioner on.
    b. Turn the engine off.
    c. Fill the tires with air.

You can save electricity by turning off appliances that you're not using.

Answers: 1. c ; 2. b

3. Which of these activities does not save energy?

    a. turning down the heat when your home is empty
    b. taking the bus
    c. leaving the TV on when you're not using it

4. Which of these activities does not save water?

    a. turning off the faucet while brushing your teeth
    b. washing your hands with cold water, not warm water
    c. taking shorter showers

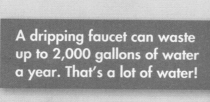
A dripping faucet can waste up to 2,000 gallons of water a year. That's a lot of water!

Answers: 3. c.; 4. b.

5. What helps to preserve forests?

    a. cutting down trees without replanting
    b. carrying your lunch in paper bags
    c. using scrap paper for math and doodling

6. What could you do to save food?

    a. Eat when you're not hungry.
    b. Save leftovers for a snack.
    c. Take more food than you can eat.

Recycling batteries or using rechargeable batteries is good for the environment.

7. You grow out of your favorite pair of jeans. How can they be recycled?

    a. Donate them to a charity.
    b. Keep them folded in a drawer.
    c. Throw them away.

Answers: 5. c; 6. b; 7. a

An adult can help you find out how your local community recycles.

RECYCLE

8. You're at the park with your friends. You've finished a bottle of juice, but there's no recycling bin to put it in. You don't want to pollute. What can you do?

a. Put it in a regular trash can.
b. Take it home and recycle it.
c. Leave it on the ground.

Your Environmental
Genius Score

6–8 You're an environmental genius!
3–5 Someone needs to introduce you to a recycling bin!
0–2 Look out, environment!

Answer: 8. b

CHANGING NATURE

4 You 2 Do

Word Play

These words got jumbled going over the Hoover Dam. Rearrange the letters to make words from the stories you read.

RECA
ANONTIMCETA
RIVETH
PRETOOM

Making Connections

What can we do to protect natural resources?

On Paper

Why are conserving and recycling important?

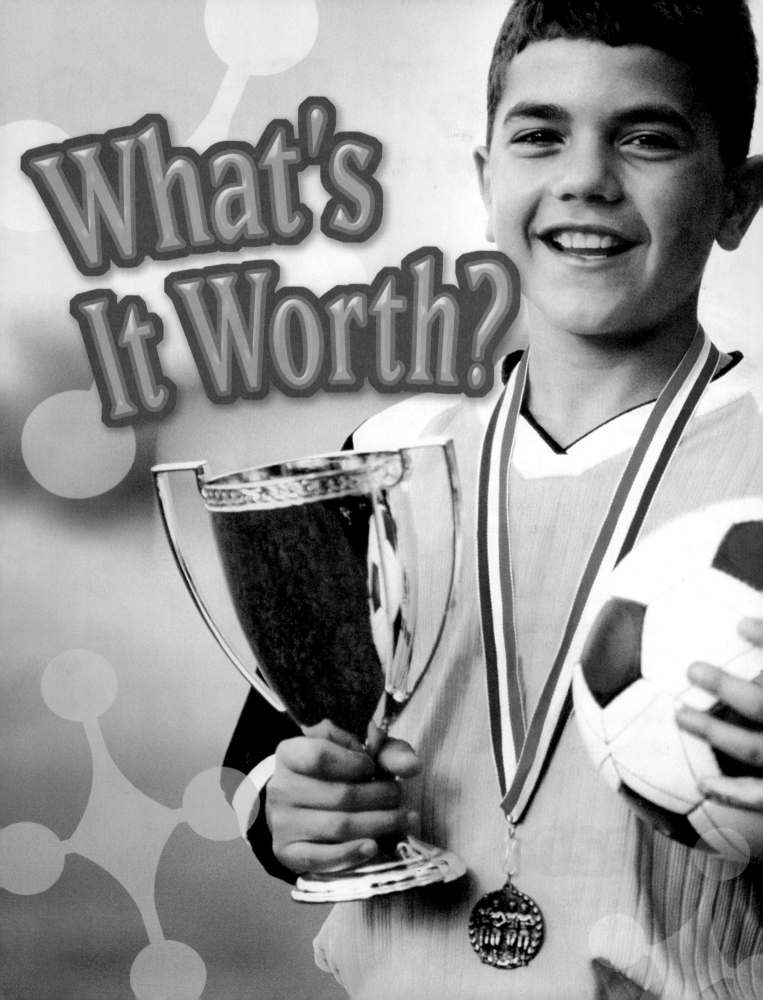

What's It Worth?

Contents

What's It Worth?

Choose an activity and explore this week's concept—Valuables!

Words 2 the Wise

Valuables are things that mean a lot to us. The value of something doesn't always have to do with money. As you read, think about what is valuable to you.

Let's Explore

Treasures

What's more valuable—a new car or a basketball? A new car, of course! But wait! You can't drive yet! Then maybe a basketball is worth more to you.

There are other ways to tell how much something is worth than by how much it costs. Some things are worth more than money could buy.

You can't always measure the value of something by its price.

Trip Around the World

Skateboard

Diamond Ring

Which would be worth more to you?

A new car may cost more money, but the price tag on something doesn't always tell its true value. What if you owned a diamond ring that your great-grandmother gave you? Yes, it's worth a lot of cash. But you would never sell it because it means a lot to you. Memories that go along with something give it more value than its price alone.

WAGNER, PITTSBURG

Do you collect anything? Some people collect baseball cards. Some people collect stamps. Collections of things may not be worth money. But they have value to the person who collects them.

Sometimes collections are worth lots of money. Many things that people collect become more valuable over time. Those baseball cards or toys you own might be worth something in the future!

This baseball card is very rare. It's worth over $1 million!

What is the value of a classic car? It can be worth lots and lots of money!

What is the value of family and friends?

The same is true for old and rare items. They're worth more because there are not enough for everyone who wants them.

So what's worth more—a new car or a basketball? There is no correct answer. A better question is, "How important is it to you?"

EVER-CHANGING MONEY

by DANIEL SCHAFER

What do goats, shells, beads, animal hides, and a basket of wheat have in common? In past times, people used each of them as currency just like we use money today.

TRADING

Long ago, people would exchange one kind of goods for another when they traded. They didn't use currency or money. This was called barter. It may have happened like this:

Farmer: I have wheat, but no bowl to grind it.

Bowl Maker: I have many bowls, but no wheat to grind.

Both: Let's trade!

When people started to barter their goods, each item traded had a different value.

Let's say you grow oranges, but you want some strawberries. A basket of berries is worth four oranges to you. The person selling the berries thinks they are worth six oranges. You barter and finally trade five oranges for the strawberries. Later, people found a different way to exchange goods. They used shells.

Will you give me your apple if I give you my carrots? Lots of kids barter.

SHELLS AS MONEY

Can you imagine paying for your lunch with shells? It seems strange that shells would be accepted as money. But around 1200 B.C., people in China began bartering goods for shells.

When you bought something, you paid with shells. And when you sold your goods, you would take shells as payment. Everyone agreed to use shells to buy and sell goods. Shells were now used as currency.

Shells like these are found in the Pacific and Indian Oceans.

SHELLS LEAD TO COINS

Around 1000 B.C. people in China made shells from metals such as bronze and copper. This was the first metal currency. By 500 B.C. metal currency spread to other countries. People began stamping rounded coins with important images and designs. These coins were made of more valuable metals such as silver and gold.

Today a dime is worth ten cents, and a nickel is five cents. Back then each metal coin also had a set monetary value.

You can see many old coins like these displayed in museums.

People also used shells as currency in North America. Native Americans valued wampum. Wampum is beads made of ground up shells.

In the 1700s Europeans in North America exchanged wampum for food, tools, and canoes. Wampum was used until the 1800s. By then the use of metal coins and paper bills had become common. However, people in China had already been using coins and bills for centuries!

Wampum beads were made from grinding and polishing shells.

A general store on an Indian reservation in New Mexico

CURRENCY TIME LINE

9000-6000 B.C.	animals, fruits and vegetables
1200 B.C.	shells
1000 B.C.	metal shells
600-300 B.C	first round metal coins
900 A.D.	first paper money used in China
1600 A.D.	paper money used in Europe
1700 A.D.	wampum common in North America
Today	credit and debit cards
Future	Will cash be used at all?

CHINA AND PAPER MONEY

Metal coins were heavy. They were difficult to carry. During the tenth century, people in China solved this problem. They made paper money.

But people didn't think paper was as valuable as gold or silver. How could someone with a five-dollar bill know it was worth that amount? What if the bank would not accept the paper? How would you get paid?

Money from around the world comes in different sizes, shapes, and designs.

Paper money was like a promise. It meant the bank promised to pay the monetary amount in gold. Banks kept gold and silver on hand. For example, if a person gave the bank five dollars, the bank would give the person five dollars worth of gold.

Now credit cards and other payment choices make it easy to buy goods without giving money. So how will you pay—with the swipe of a card or with cash?

People make more purchases with electronic payments than with cash.

WHAT DO YOU THINK?

How has money changed over time?

Stone Soup

by Janet Ishida · illustrated by Julie Downing

Jack picked the last strawberry. He couldn't wait to share the juicy treat with his family! Winter had been hard last year, and food was scarce.

I wonder if there are more berries down the path, he thought. So instead of heading home, he walked further into the wilderness. The berries smelled so sweet!

The bear that charged out of the woods thought so too. Jack threw his strawberries at the bear and ran for his life!

After a while, Jack came upon a village. He was lost and hungry. The empty pot was heavy, but it was too important to leave behind.

Jack knocked on the door of the first cottage, and a kindly looking woman answered.

"Good day, ma'am. Will you share a hot meal with me? Then I will be on my way."

The woman shook her head sadly. "We don't have enough food to share. Try the next cottage."

The answer at each cottage was the same. No one had any food to share. Jack was lost, hungry, and tired from carrying the heavy pot.

Then Jack had an idea! Jack filled the old pot with water and made a fire. He set the pot over the fire, and then he chose the perfect stone. Not too big. Not too small. He brushed it off on his sleeve, and he dropped it into the pot.

Jack used a long stick to stir the pot. After a while, a little girl peeked from her window. "What are you making?" she called out.

"Stone soup," Jack said, drawing a deep breath. "It's almost ready! I just need a few potatoes."

The little girl came out of her cottage with three big potatoes, which Jack added to the pot. "Doesn't it smell good?" said Jack.

The little girl nodded. "Too bad we don't have some carrots," she said.

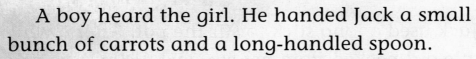

A boy heard the girl. He handed Jack a small bunch of carrots and a long-handled spoon.

"Thank you," said Jack as he added the carrots to the pot and stirred it with the spoon. "Our stone soup will be delicious!"

The children both nodded. "It's a shame we don't have some corn."

Two doors opened, and hands held out corn. Jack stirred the corn in with the other vegetables and took a little taste.

"This is so tasty!" Jack declared. "If only I had a few pieces of dried meat . . ."

Three people came with strips of meat, and into the pot they went! As the villagers were sniffing the aroma of the soup, they smiled.

Jack stirred the pot, and he gave the little boy a small taste. "Quite good!" the boy exclaimed. "But a little salt and pepper would add flavor."

One villager brought a scoop of salt and dropped it into the pot. Someone else added pepper, and Jack stirred the stone soup. He had a little taste.

"This needs something more, but I'm not sure what," he said.

One child spoke up. "Would a handful of wild onions make it taste better?"

Jack nodded. Several children ran to their homes. Some did not have onions, so they dropped other vegetables, spices, and bits of dried meat into the pot.

As Jack cooked, the villagers smacked their lips. When the soup was done, they all ate until they were full. The people drew a map in the sandy dirt to show him the way home.

Afterward, Jack took the stone from the pot. He wiped it off, and he gave it to the little girl. "Keep this as an important reminder," he said. "It will keep hunger from your village." Then he picked up his pot and took the path home.

What Do You Think?

How did villagers treat Jack in the beginning and in the end? Why did they change?

What's My

$1,500,000 $800,000

Try this quick quiz. Read the descriptions and choose the price of each item from above.

Only about 80 "Inverted Jenny" stamps exist today. They are worth a lot of money because they are rare.

1. Postage Stamp

I am the "Inverted Jenny" stamp. The U.S. government accidentally printed the airplane upside down. What's my value?

2. Ruby Slippers

I am one of four pairs of ruby slippers that Judy Garland wore when she played Dorothy in *The Wizard of Oz*. What's my value?

These ruby-red slippers have become very valuable since 1939.

Answers:
1. $800,000
2. $1,500,000

80

Value?

$130,000 $608 million $6.99

3. Comic Book

I am the first *Superman* comic book. I was printed in 1938. I am in excellent condition. What's my value?

Comic books that have the first appearance of popular characters are very valuable. Less than 100 copies of the first *Superman* comic book exist today.

4. Paperback book

I am any popular paperback book. Children and adults around the world have read me. What's my value?

5. Mona Lisa

I am one of Leonardo da Vinci's most famous paintings. My smile is known around the world. What's my value?

Mona Lisa, 1503–1505, Leonardo da Vinci

People have been making copies of the *Mona Lisa* since the 1500s. You might recognize the portrait from posters or cards, but there is only one original painting.

Answers:
3. $130,000;
4. $6.99;
5. $608 million

4 Fun 2 Do

Word Play

Match each concept word with the letter of the word that best describes it.

1. currency   a. trade
2. barter   b. value
3. worth   c. money

Making Connections

We learned how shells and stones can be valuable. Explain what makes these and other unlikely items valuable.

On Paper

What is valuable to you? Why?

Answers to Word Play: 1. currency, c; 2. barter, a; 3. worth, b.

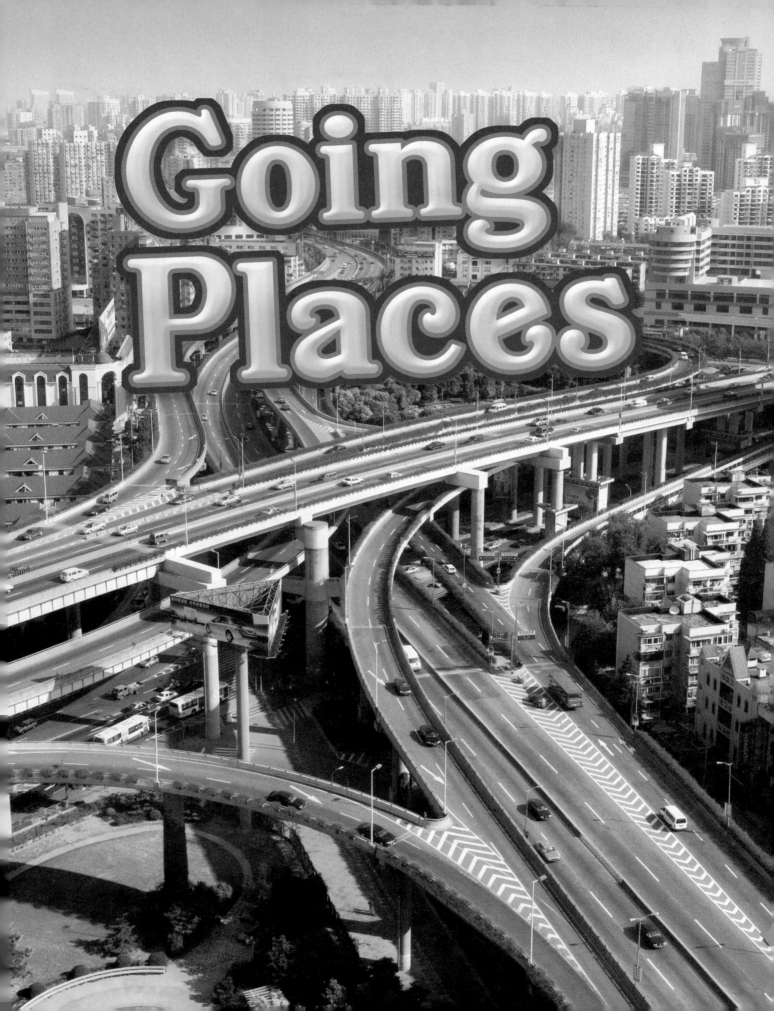

Going Places

Contents

Going Places

Words 2 the Wise

How we **travel** depends on where we need to go. We might walk, or we might ride in a car. The ways we go places have changed over time. As you read, think about the different ways you travel.

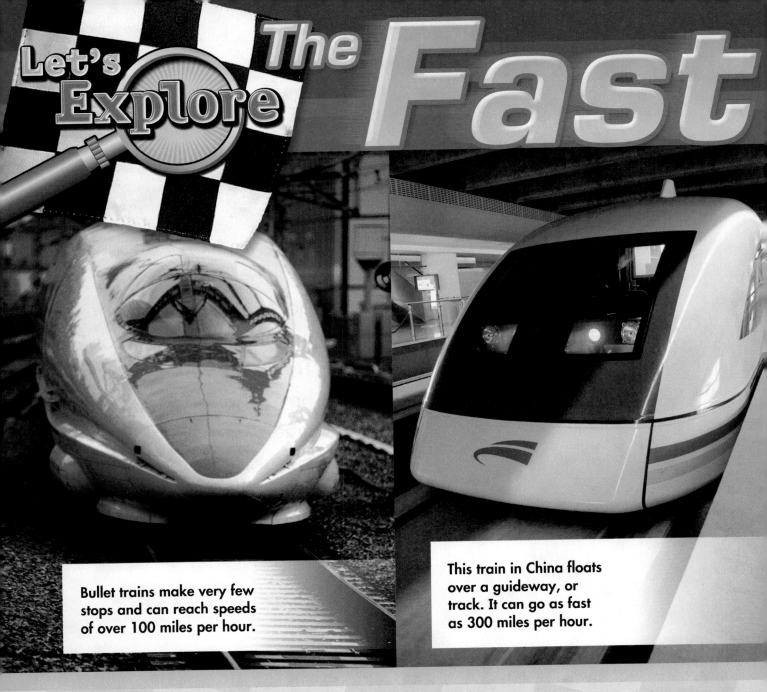

Let's Explore The Fast

Bullet trains make very few stops and can reach speeds of over 100 miles per hour.

This train in China floats over a guideway, or track. It can go as fast as 300 miles per hour.

Airplanes can take you to the other side of the world in a few hours. But travel hasn't always been this fast. Early steam ships took weeks to sail across the Atlantic Ocean.

In 1838 a ship called the *Sirius* (SEER-ee-uhs) raced another ship. It set sail from London, England. The crew aboard the *Sirius* won the race. They reached New York in eighteen days. Back then, that was fast!

Lane

On the German autobahn, cars can travel up to 130 miles per hour.

The Boeing 777 travels about 615 miles per hour.

Today people travel even faster. A jet airplane takes about seven hours to fly from London to New York. The passengers on the *Sirius* would be astonished at such speed!

They would be even more amazed if they could drive a car 130 miles per hour. This happens on the German highway called the autobahn. They could also ride a bullet train in Japan or France. These travel over 100 miles per hour.

Getting Around

by Ujvala Khot

How do you get where you need to go? Do you hop on your bike or scooter? Cars, buses, trains, and planes are not the only ways to get around.

At different times and places in the world, people have used all types of conveyances. Many travelers walked to get where they were going. But some people reached their destinations by having other people drive or carry them.

Some people in China ride in sedan chairs (left). Above, horses pull a carriage.

The Rickshaw

Early rickshaws were two-wheeled carriages with long handles. You climbed in the seat, and the driver pulled you through traffic.

Rickshaws may have been invented in France, but they were used mostly in Japan. The Japanese name for a rickshaw is *jinrikisha* (jeen-REE-kee-shah). This means "human-powered vehicle." In the 1870s the rickshaw was the main form of transportation in Japan. Soon the rickshaw spread throughout the rest of Asia.

Drivers pull passengers in a rickshaw.

Old-style rickshaws are still used in some Asian cities. But in most other cities, rickshaws have changed a lot.

Some carry two or three passengers and look like bicycle carriages. New rickshaws with motors make it easier for the drivers. These simple conveyances are a popular way for people in crowded cities to get to their destinations. They are not very fast, but they are cheaper than taxis.

Auto rickshaws are used to get around in India.

Cycle rickshaws are still used in many parts of Asia.

Sedan Chairs for Hire

The sedan chair was invented in Asia. By 1634, the first sedan chairs appeared in England. Chairmen, or sedan chair carriers, had to get a license to operate them. People hired sedans the way we hire taxi cabs today. When the weather was bad, passengers were carried right into their homes!

Sedan chair races are held every year in Hong Kong to raise money for local charities. Boy Scouts in England also run sedan chair races.

Sedan chairs are no longer used as a main source of transportation.

Horse and Carriage Travel

Before automobiles were invented, many people traveled in horse-drawn carriages. Carriages are covered coaches that protect the passengers from rain and wind.

The Queen of England has several coaches that she often uses. The royal family travels in the Gold State Coach on the day a new king or queen is crowned.

A horse-drawn carriage

The Gold State Coach

The Gold State Coach was built in 1762. It weighs four tons. It is so heavy that eight horses must pull it. Footmen walk alongside the horses and guide the coach.

The Queen does not ride in a coach all of the time. Most of the time she travels in a car.

Sedan chairs and coaches may not be used for everyday travel anymore, but sometimes they are brought out for special occasions.

Go, Baby! Go!

South American women have carried babies in cloth slings for hundreds of years. To make a sling, the mother ties a large piece of fabric over one shoulder. It becomes a cloth cradle. When she carries the baby inside it, her hands are free. In African cultures, the sling is tied so the baby sits on a mother's hip.

Some Native American mothers used cradle boards. Babies were placed on a flat board and wrapped with cloth.

Mothers around the world travel with their babies wherever they go!

How Do YOU Get Around?

Would it surprise you to see the Gold State Coach on your street? Could a rickshaw driver take you to school? Or would a skateboard or bicycle be a better way to travel?

People need ways to get from one place to another. Different conveyances have solved their transportation problems. What conveyances do you think will be invented in the next 100 years?

What Do You Think?

What makes the conveyances from this selection unusual?

From Sea to SHINING

Wagons for Travel

Walking is a fine way to travel, unless you need to get somewhere fast or haul something. For hundreds of years Native American people walked around the United States. Later they rode horses.

Then in the early 1800s settlers began using big, heavy Conestoga (kahn-uh-STOH-guh) wagons for transportation. Horses pulled Conestoga wagons. People could now haul heavier freight. The wagons were useful for many years.

Wagons once carried people and freight across the U.S.

SEA

by John Ryan

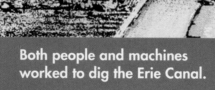
Both people and machines worked to dig the Erie Canal.

A Canal to the West

Wagons could travel across dirt and grass. But it was hard to go over mountains or through the wilderness in a wagon. People started to move goods up and down rivers. But the rivers didn't always lead to where the people needed to go.

The solution was to build canals. Canals are man-made waterways that connect lakes, rivers, or oceans. The most heavily used canal in North America was the Erie Canal.

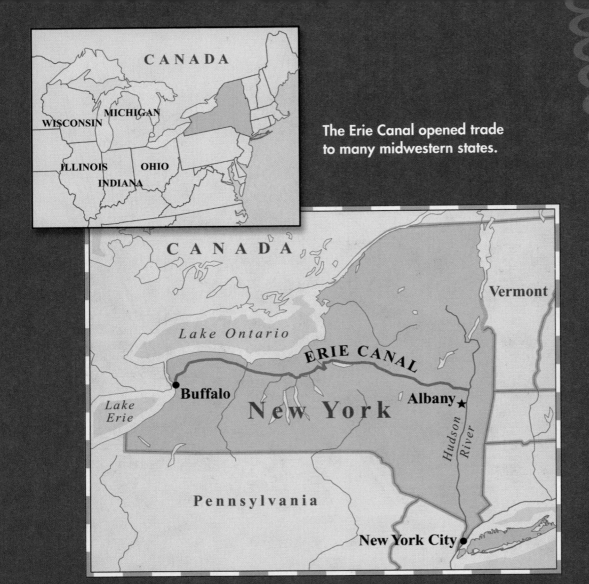

The Erie Canal opened trade to many midwestern states.

The Erie Canal was opened in 1825. It connected the Hudson River in eastern New York state with Lake Erie in the western part. Rough terrain and wilderness no longer prevented people from going west.

The Erie Canal gave people a way to reach other states. Travelers could now go from New York City, through the Great Lakes, and into the middle of the country.

The Railroad Connects East and West

Today travelers can drive, take a train, or fly from one side of the country to the other. But in the 1800s there was no direct way to travel across the continent.

In 1869 workers finished laying tracks for a transcontinental railroad in Promontory, Utah. The Central Pacific Railroad from the east and the Union Pacific Railroad from the west were connected. Now trains could carry people and freight from coast to coast.

Over 4,000 workers built the transcontinental railroad.

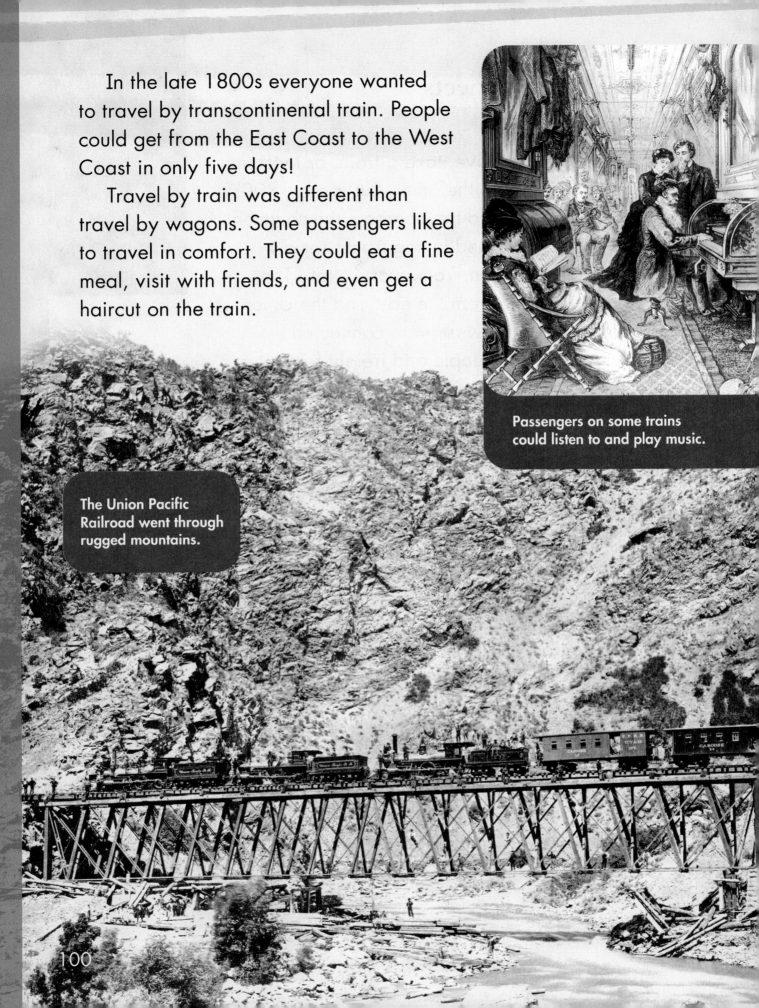

In the late 1800s everyone wanted to travel by transcontinental train. People could get from the East Coast to the West Coast in only five days!

Travel by train was different than travel by wagons. Some passengers liked to travel in comfort. They could eat a fine meal, visit with friends, and even get a haircut on the train.

Passengers on some trains could listen to and play music.

The Union Pacific Railroad went through rugged mountains.

Cars and Roads

Early cars were powered by steam, electricity, and gas. People liked the gas-powered cars because they were dependable and ready when they were needed. But most roads were old wagon roads. People needed better highways. The first highway was the Abraham Lincoln Highway. It ran from New York to San Francisco.

More new highways were built across the continent. People could drive on smooth roads instead of dirt roads.

Henry Ford sits in an early car that he designed.

Interstate Highway System

Highways were just the beginning. During World War II, General Dwight Eisenhower saw the autobahn (AW-toh-bahn) in Germany. The autobahn is made up of highways that have many lanes of traffic in each direction. A short wall separates the lanes. Eisenhower noticed that the autobahn helped people travel quickly between cities.

Eisenhower became President in 1953. He wanted to build highways like the autobahn in the United States.

In 1990 the Interstate Highway System was officially renamed the Dwight D. Eisenhower National System of Interstate and Defense Highways.

102

In 1956 workers began building the Interstate Highway System. The U.S. would have about 35,000 miles of modern highways by 1975. The system has grown throughout the years. In 2004 the system had grown to over 46,800 miles of roads.

Transportation is always changing. Narrow paths were good for walking. Those paths grew into wider roads for wagons. When cars became common, the roads grew into highways. What changes in transportation do you see?

The Interstate Highway System has altered the way Americans travel.

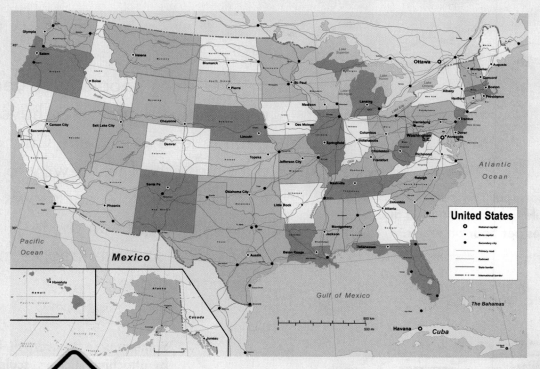

WHAT DO YOU THINK?

How has crossing the United States changed over the years?

Cool Cars

This sports car can travel at 100 miles per hour on land and 30 miles per hour on water.

Ever since people have been able to afford cars, they have been in love with them. Cars are a lot more than just a way to get to a destination. A car shows what kind of person owns it. That's why so many people make their cars unique.

Some people decorate their cars by attaching stickers, sculptures, bottle caps, or sea shells to the outsides of them.

Chitty Chitty Bang Bang is a movie about a professor who invents a flying car that can drive itself!

In the 1960s cars became an important part of entertainment too. The stars in movies often drove unique cars. *Chitty Chitty Bang Bang* was one movie that starred a car.

The Aston Martin DB5 is famous for being the first car to appear in a popular spy movie.

GOING PLACES

105

Cities all across the country have automobile shows. People can show different kinds of cars.

Some people are wild about antique cars. They collect them and try to keep them in good condition. And they drive them, of course! Cars have become an important part of American culture.

People are always creating new designs for cars. Will you see this one rolling down the highway in the future?

This pink Cadillac was owned by the famous singer Elvis Presley.

Many people feel that cars tell something about their personalities. They think that cars are plain until they put their own special touches onto them. How would a car that you design look?

Some people use trucks like these to travel on paved or rocky roads.

4 2 Do

Word Play

Unscramble the word below. How many smaller words can you make from it?

o o a a i p n n r r t t t s

Making Connections

You read about many ways to get around. How would you like to travel? Why?

On Paper

Design a dream machine for traveling across an ocean or a continent. Write a description of your machine.

Influences

88 89 90 91 92 93 94 95 96 97 98

4 News at 10

Contents

Influences

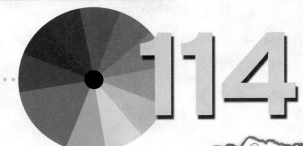

Words 2 the Wise

We see and hear many **influences** every day. Advertisements are influences that affect our decisions to buy products. As you read think about how advertisements influence you.

Sunshine Fresh Oranges
5 for $1

Let's Explore Ads

An advertisement, or ad, is a way for companies to tell you about their products. Ads can be on TV, radio, or in newspapers. Advertisements try to persuade you to buy products. Have you ever seen or heard an advertisement that made you want to buy something?

Advertisers use famous people to influence people to buy things. They hope you'll want to use these products because famous people use them.

I wear these. You should too.

Advertisers use famous people to say that a product is good. This is called a testimonial (test-uh-MOH-nee-uhl).

Some commercials claim* that you'll miss out if you don't use a product. The ad is really saying, "Everyone is buying the product. You should too!"

Some ads are filled with words that don't tell you anything about the product. Others claim that magic will happen if you use their products.

See what techniques ads use to persuade you.

*claim say strongly that something is true

Advertisers use words to make us feel a certain way. Many times these words are not related to the product. These are called loaded words.

Sometimes advertisers want us to think we are the only ones not buying a certain product. This is called the bandwagon.

Drink Sunny Side

A taste of pure sunshine!

Everyone's buying HairRight!

HairRight

Advertisers pay to play their commercials on TV.

Hidden Messages

by Danielle Hammelef

Have you ever felt your mood change when you listened to a song? Do you have a favorite color to wear when you are happy? Music, color, and images send powerful messages. They often influence our bodies and minds.

Color Messages

People use colors to describe feelings. Maybe you've heard a sad person say, "I'm feeling blue." When people are jealous, we say that they are "green with envy."

Some colors have more than one meaning. Red gives us energy and signals a warning.

114

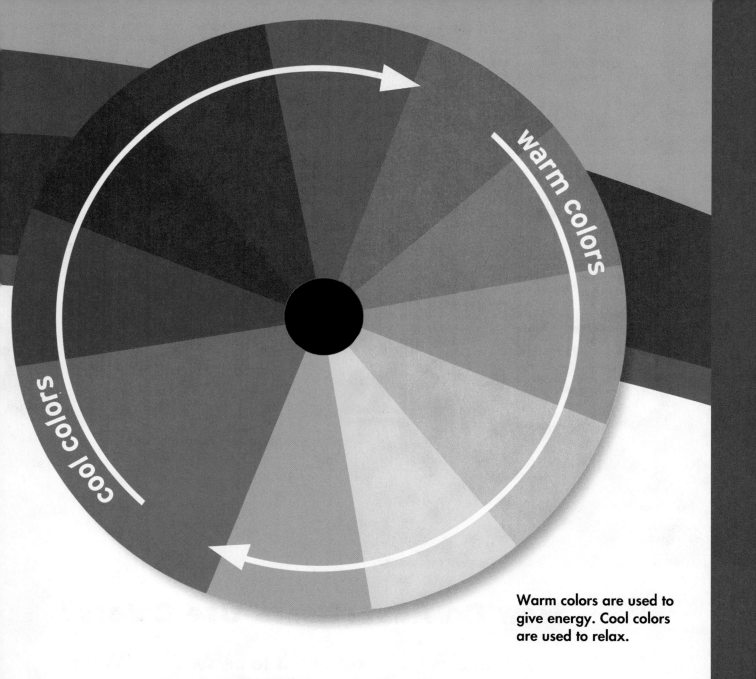

warm colors

cool colors

Warm colors are used to give energy. Cool colors are used to relax.

Colors influence our feelings. Warm colors, such as red, yellow, and orange, give us energy.

Cool colors, such as green, blue, and purple, signal relaxation. Cool colors help our bodies relax.

Being around too many of these colors may have the opposite effect. Too much red can make people impatient. Too much blue can make people gloomy.

Think about the colors you choose for clothes or for a drawing. Why do you like those colors?

Restaurant owners choose colors that influence their customers.

How Do Advertisers Use Colors?

Advertisers use colors in ads to persuade us. What colors would appear in an advertisement for a sports drink? People that play sports are energetic, so these ads usually have reds and yellows.

Fast food restaurants are often red and yellow. These energetic colors make customers feel hungry and eat fast.

Other restaurants might be green and blue. These relaxing colors make diners want to stay longer and order more from the menu.

A person's mood can change with the music.

Music Messages

Like color, music is everywhere. Music can make our hearts beat faster or our bodies relax. Music can make us happy or sad.

Movies, television shows, and radio use music to influence people. Think about a scary scene in a movie. Did the music get louder and louder? Did your heart beat faster and faster? Music can control our moods.

Music and jingles are ways that advertisers persuade consumers to buy their products.

Have you heard a jingle* with an advertisement on TV or radio? Sometimes hearing a jingle makes you hum it all day. Commercials play catchy music to help you remember the product.

Stores use music to influence buyers. The next time you go to a store, notice the music that is playing in the background. When happy music is played, people might feel happy. If people feel happy, they may feel like buying more.

*jingle short, simple, catchy song

Our brains must make sense of many messages during movies.

Hidden Messages

Commercials use color and music to convince you to buy the products. Sellers also use hidden messages. These are messages that you don't know your mind is listening to.

Hidden messages can be words or pictures. They can be used in advertisements, movies, commercials, and stores. In the 1950s people experimented with hidden messages. A businessman named James Vicary said that he experimented with these messages during a movie.

How many messages are coming at YOU every day?

James Vicary said he had flashed *eat popcorn* onto the screen many times while people were watching a movie. The messages flashed off so fast that people didn't realize they were seeing them. Later he said that more popcorn was sold during that movie.

People were nervous when they found out about James Vicary's experiment. Eventually, he confessed that the experiment was a fake. Yet people believed that advertisers were trying to control them.

Advertisers use symbols to send another kind of hidden message. White jackets make people think of doctors. Actors wear white jackets in ads about medicine to convince people that a doctor is telling them to use the product.

You Decide!

Do advertisers persuade people with hidden messages? Some scientists say that hidden messages work. Others say they have no effect.

The next time you watch commercials or read advertisements, notice the colors, music, and images. How are they trying to persuade you?

What Do You Think?

How do ads persuade people?

INFLUENCES

THE EDGE

BY HENRY BELLFONT • ILLUSTRATED BY MAURIE J. MANNING

"Short guys like us need an edge," Will told Mike. They were planning to try out for the basketball team at Meyer School.

Mike frowned. "Edge? What do you mean?"

"This!" said Will, grinning. He whipped a magazine out of his backpack. "Look at these beauties," he said.

The advertisement for Launchers took up a whole page of the sports magazine. The shoes were blue and yellow. They claimed to put anyone into outer space.

Mike saw himself in Launchers, flying through the air over the heads of the other team. Slam dunk!

"Wow," he breathed. Then he saw the $200 price in small print.

When Mike got home, Uncle Tim was there. He and Grandma Deb owned Five Points Diner, where Uncle Tim was chef and Grandma was hostess.

"Ready for tryouts, Mike?" Uncle Tim asked.

"That's what I have to talk to you about, Uncle Tim . . ."

Uncle Tim's eyebrows went up.

"I need Launchers so I'll make the team," said Mike.

"How much are they?" asked Uncle Tim.

"They're $200," Mike said. "If you'll help pay, I'll work off the rest at the diner."

"Getting sucked in by an ad, huh? You're pretty gullible if you are."

"It's just that these shoes are important," Mike replied.

"OK," said Uncle Tim. "I'll loan you the money. But you'll learn if products or practice makes good players!"

The next day Uncle Tim took Mike to the mall. *These shoes look even better on my feet than in the advertisement,* Mike thought.

That night Mike called Will.

"I have them!" he said. "Now I can do jumpers so high they'll have to scrape me off the ceiling!"

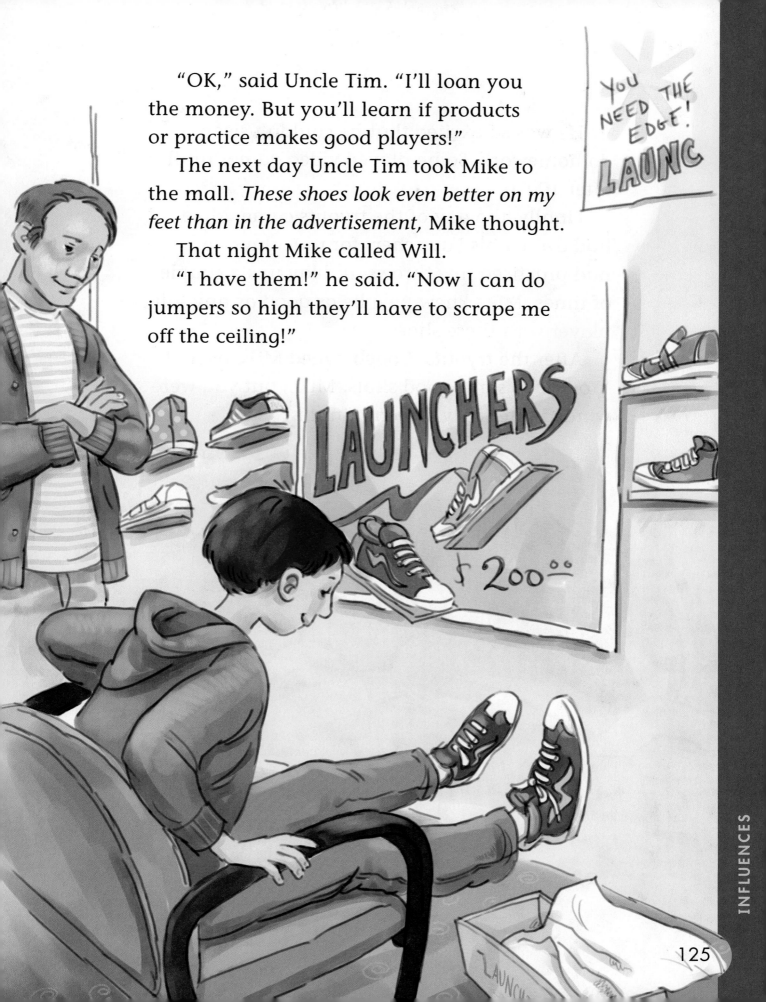

YOU NEED THE EDGE! LAUNC

LAUNCHERS

$200⁰⁰

125

He was so excited that he couldn't sleep or do homework. So he played video games until after 10 P.M.

Finally, the day of the tryouts came. Mike had owned his Launchers for nine days, and had practiced free throws and lay ups a couple of times. Mike knew he'd be as good as any tall player with these shoes.

After the tryouts, Coach called Mike over. "You have some good shots, Mike, but you were winded after only fifteen minutes."

LAUNCHERS
I'VE GOT THE EDGE!

"I'll give you a chance, but you need to practice to keep your place on this team," warned Coach.

When he got home, Mike shouted, "These shoes gave me my edge!"

"Well, you did practice," said Uncle Tim. "Right?"

"Some," said Mike.

"Some?" His uncle stared. "I'm not gullible. Shoes don't replace practice. You might be warming the bench instead of playing."

Practices began. Mike wore his Launchers during practice every day.

127

One day Uncle Tim stopped at practice. "How's Mike doing, Coach?" he asked.

Coach smiled. "At first he wasn't focusing. Now when he gets around a block, he creates his own shots! On Saturday we play our big rival, Mapleton. Mike looks ready!"

But on Saturday when Mike opened his bag in the locker room, the Launchers were gone. His stomach clenched. He had taken them out to show Will last night. He had forgotten to put them back!

How could he play without his edge? The next minute the team was on the court. All his practice paid off. Mike didn't let the other guards stuff him. He made jumpers and free throws. Mike's team won by three points!

Suddenly, the team was together giving high fives. Mike glanced down at his ragged shoes. Then he looked up at the sweaty, cheering faces. He knew what the real edge was!

WHAT DO YOU THINK?

What did Mike do after he bought his new shoes?

Would **YOU** Buy It?

Advertisements use these techniques to try to persuade us.

Bandwagon says that everyone is buying a product.

Loaded Words are words like "enormous" and "outstanding." They don't really tell about the product.

Testimonial is when a famous person claims that a product is the best.

Read these examples.
Which technique is being used?

1. Surround your feet in these incredibly soft slippers. You'll think you're walking on clouds!

    a. bandwagon
    b. loaded words
    c. testimonial

2. If you want to look good while preventing sun damage, wear this sunscreen. It's what every cool kid is wearing to the beach.

    a. bandwagon
    b. loaded words
    c. testimonial

3. I am a superstar with the brightest smile around. Do you want a smile like mine? Buy Briteen toothpaste!

  a. bandwagon
  b. loaded words
  c. testimonial

4. Choose from six sassy styles and designs. These hats are the best! You'll be toasty warm all winter long!

  a. bandwagon
  b. loaded words
  c. testimonial

5. I am the greatest athlete in the world. I use Smell Away deodorant. If you don't, you might as well not use anything.

   a. bandwagon
   b. loaded words
   c. testimonial

6. Does someone have to tickle you or poke you each morning? Hundreds of kids wake up to their favorite songs every day with this alarm clock. Now you can too!

   a. bandwagon
   b. loaded words
   c. testimonial

Answers to Would You Buy It?
1. b—loaded words;
2. a—bandwagon;
3. c—testimonial;
4. b—loaded words;
5. c—testimonial;
6. a—bandwagon.

4 YOU 2 Do

Word Play

Follow the directions to make new words. Then make a sentence from the words. Do you think the sentence is true?

ADS

Replace *s* with *vertise.*

Add *ments.*

PURSE

Switch *u* and *e.*

Add *ade* to the end.

What sentence did you create?

Making Connections

How did the makers of Launchers persuade Mike?

On Paper

What is your favorite food? Create an advertisement to persuade someone to buy it. Be sure to add a drawing.

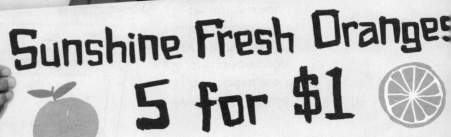

Sunshine Fresh Oranges
5 for $1

Glossary

a·cre (ā/ kər), *NOUN.* a unit of area used to measure land. An acre is equal to 43,560 square feet: *The city bought 10 acres of land for a new park.* PL. **a·cres.**

ad·van·ta·geous (ad/ vən tā/ jəs), *ADJECTIVE.* favorable; helpful: *It can be advantageous to live across the street from the school you attend.*

ad·ver·tise·ment (ad/ vər tīz/ mənt), *NOUN.* a paid announcement telling about some product, service, or need: *The toothpaste advertisement featured a famous person.*

a in hat	ō in open	sh in she
ā in age	ȯ in all	th in thin
â in care	ô in order	ᴛʜ in then
ä in far	oi in oil	zh in measure
e in let	ou in out	ə =a in about
ē in equal	u in cup	ə =e in taken
ėr in term	u̇ in put	ə =i in pencil
i in it	ü in rule	ə =o in lemon
ī in ice	ch in child	ə =u in circus
o in hot	ng in long	

bar·ter (bär′ tər), *VERB.* to trade by exchanging one kind of good for another without using money; exchange: *The trapper bartered furs for supplies.*

com·mer·cial (kə mėr′ shəl), *NOUN.* an advertising message on television or radio, broadcast between or during programs: *Have you seen the commercial for that new video game?* *PL.* **com·mer·cials.**

con·tam·i·nate (kən tam′ ə nāt), *VERB.* to make something impure or spoiled by mixing it with something else; pollute: *The water was contaminated by sewage.* **con·tam·i·nates, con·tam·i·nat·ed, con·tam·i·nat·ing.**

con·trol (kən′ trōl), *VERB.* to have power or authority over; to direct: *The government controls the printing of money.* **con·trolled, control·ling.**

con·vey·ance (kən vā′ əns), *NOUN.* a thing that carries people and goods; a vehicle: *Trains and buses are public conveyances.* *PL.* **con·vey·anc·es.**

con·vince (kən vins′), VERB. to make someone believe something: *We tried to convince him to go to the movies with us.* **con·vinced, con·vinc·ing.**

cur·ren·cy (ker′ ən sē), NOUN. the money in use in a country: *Coins and paper money are currency in the United States.* PL. **cur·ren·cies.**

de·pend (di pend′), VERB. to have as a support; get help from: *Pets depend on their owners for food and shelter.*

des·ti·na·tion (des′ tə nā′ shən), NOUN. the place to which a person or thing is going or is being sent: *We used the map to find our destination.* PL. **des·ti·na·tions.**

a in hat	ō in open	sh in she
ā in age	ȯ in all	th in thin
â in care	ô in order	ŦH in then
ä in far	oi in oil	zh in measure
e in let	ou in out	ə =a in about
ē in equal	u in cup	ə =e in taken
ėr in term	u̇ in put	ə =i in pencil
i in it	ü in rule	ə =o in lemon
ī in ice	ch in child	ə =u in circus
o in hot	ng in long	

dis·ap·point·ed (dis′ ə point′ əd), ADJECTIVE. unhappiness that something failed to satisfy one's desire, expectation, or hope: *He was disappointed about the book's ending.* **dis·ap·point·ing.**

en·coun·ter (en koun′ tər), VERB.

1 to meet someone or something unexpectedly: *What if we should encounter a bear?*
2 to have to deal with something; experience: *She encountered many challenges in her new job.* **en·coun·tered, en·coun·ter·ing.**

ex·change (eks chānj′), VERB. to give something to someone in return for something else; trade: *He exchanged the tight-fitting coat for one that was a size larger.* **ex·changed, ex·chang·ing.**

freight (frāt), NOUN. the products that a train, truck, ship, or aircraft carries: *The ship carried its freight of cars across the ocean.*

gul·li·ble (gul′ ə bəl), ADJECTIVE. too ready to believe whatever people say and easy to cheat or trick: *He is so gullible that he really thought the moon was made of cheese.*

hitch (hich), NOUN. something that causes a delay or makes things more difficult: *A hitch in their plans made them miss the train.*

im·por·tant (im pôrt′ nt), ADJECTIVE. having great meaning or value: *The Mona Lisa is an important work of art.*

Mona Lisa, 1503–1505, Leonardo da Vinci

a in hat	ō in open	sh in she
ā in age	ȯ in all	th in thin
â in care	ô in order	ᵺH in then
ä in far	oi in oil	zh in measure
e in let	ou in out	ə =a in about
ē in equal	u in cup	ə =e in taken
ėr in term	u̇ in put	ə =i in pencil
i in it	ü in rule	ə =o in lemon
ī in ice	ch in child	ə =u in circus
o in hot	ng in long	

in·flu·ence (in′ flü əns),
1 *NOUN.* someone or something that gets us to think or act in a certain way: *His older brother is a good influence on him.*
2 *VERB.* to have some effect on: *What we read can influence our thinking.*

mon·e·tar·y (mon′ ə ter′ ē), *ADJECTIVE.* of or about the money of a country: *The monetary unit in the United States is the dollar.*

pas·sen·ger (pas′ n jər), *NOUN.* someone who rides in an aircraft, bus, ship, train, car, or other vehicle: *The cart carried two passengers.*
PL. **pass·en·gers.**

per·suade (pər swād′), *VERB.* to get someone to do something or to believe something: *I knew I should study, but he persuaded me to go to the movies instead.*

pre·dict (pri dikt′), *VERB.* to tell about something before it happens: *The weather service predicts rain for tomorrow.*
pre·dict·ed, pre·dict·ing.

pre·serve (pri zėrv′), VERB. to keep something from harm or change; protect: *Good nutrition helps preserve your health.*

pro·mote (prə mōt′), VERB. to try to sell something by advertising it: *The basketball star promoted the new shoe.* **pro·mot·ed, pro·mot·ing.**

I wear these. You should too.

sur·prise (sər prīz′), NOUN. something unexpected: *Our grandparents always have a surprise for us when we visit them.*

thrive (thrīv), VERB. to grow strong and healthy: *Vines can thrive in warm areas.* **thrived** or **throve, thriv·ing.**

a in hat	ō in open	sh in she
ā in age	ȯ in all	th in thin
â in care	ô in order	ŦH in then
ä in far	oi in oil	zh in measure
e in let	ou in out	ə =a in about
ē in equal	u in cup	ə =e in taken
ėr in term	u̇ in put	ə =i in pencil
i in it	ü in rule	ə =o in lemon
ī in ice	ch in child	ə =u in circus
o in hot	ng in long	

trans·con·ti·nen·tal (tran′ skon tə nen′ tl), ADJECTIVE.
crossing a continent: *The first transcontinental railroad in the U.S. was completed in 1869.*

trans·por·ta·tion (tran′ spər tā′ shən), NOUN.
1 the business of carrying people or goods: *Trains, cars, trucks, buses, and airplanes are all methods of transportation.*
2 a vehicle used to carry people or things: *A plane was the only means of transportation to the remote island.*

trav·el (trav′ əl),
1 VERB. to go from one place to another; journey: *She will travel to Europe this summer.*
2 NOUN. going in airplanes, trains, ships, cars, and so on, from one place to another: *His job as a flight attendant involves lots of travel.*